MW01152893

LEARN TO PLAY
BLUEGRASS
DOBRO® GUITAR

By Ken Eidson & Tom Swatzell

DOBRO® is a registered trademark owned by Original Musical Instrument Company, a division of Gibson Guitar Corporation. DOBRO® refers to a particular brand of guitar. The generic name of the style of guitar playing contained in this book is "resonator guitar" or "resophonic guitar."

Online Audio   www.melbay.com/93968BCDEB

AUDIO CONTENTS

© 1984 BY MEL BAY PUBLICATIONS, INC., PACIFIC, MO 63069.
ALL RIGHTS RESERVED. INTERNATIONAL COPYRIGHT SECURED. B.M.I. MADE AND PRINTED IN U.S.A.
Visit us on the Web at http://www.melbay.com — E-mail us at email@melbay.com

1 2 3 4 5 6 7 8 9 0

AUTHORS' NOTE

Since our first DOBRO book with Mel Bay (*Country DOBRO Guitar Styles*) came out in 1974, we have seen a tremendous increase in the popularity of the DOBRO guitar. We are proud to note that a fair share of that popularity has been due to the presence of our book in the music stores, enabling pickers to study the instrument by *eye* as well as by *ear* (the more usual way). This book *Learn to Play Bluegrass Dobro Guitar* reflects the current interest in Bluegrass music as well as the technical requirements needed when a DOBRO player sits in with a Bluegrass band. Some of these tunes are right out of the Bluegrass repertory, while others are less often heard. We have tried to give the student good technical information (ammunition, if you will) so that he or she will be able to play not only the tunes in this book, but will also have a head start on adapting whatever material comes their way to make the sounds that fit with a Bluegrass group. To that end, you will find right hand rolls and rhythm strums, slides, hammers-on and slant bars, harmonics and tremolos. Take the licks with our blessing, but also try to add them to the other songs you play; this will make your own picking richer and more interesting for the listener.

We would like to dedicate this book to the late Mr. E.E. Dopera who passed away in November 1976. Ed, with his brothers John and Rudy, had a lot to do with the early days and the recent days of DOBRO. It was he who initially encouraged us to write a book about the instrument.

You will find that the songs in this book get progressively more difficult. This is not to say that you shouldn't skip around if you want to; but a careful study of the whole book, in order, will reward the diligent student with a world of DOBRO knowledge. It has been our privilege to share this knowledge with you.

Tom Swatzell
Ken Eidson

Ken Eidson

Tom Swatzell

2

Table of Contents

°Dobro is a registered trademark of O.M.I., Inc. Used by Permission.

For information concerning tapes of the songs in this book write to:
Ken Eidson, 2121 Linneman Street, Glenview, Illinois 60025

NOTE READING AND TABLATURE

This book is designed to get you started playing DOBRO in the slide, or Hawaiian style of steel guitar that is increasingly popular today. Bluegrass and Country-Western musicians (not to mention musicians in the pop fields) use Dobro guitars. If you are thinking of buying a Dobro or if you already own one, here are the things you will need to know in order to play.

I. Note Reading

Even though it is not absolutely necessary to read music in order to make music, your learning time will be cut considerably if you can be an independent, literate musician, so why not learn to read the notes now?

The notes for DOBRO (and other instruments too) are written on a five-line staff:

The treble clef sign, 𝄞 -shows that you are not reading bass notes, and it also shows you where G is: on the second line from the bottom. The tail of the clef sign curls around the second line:

Notes on the staff are alphabetical (A-G) as long as you proceed from line to space, like this:

A   B   C   D   E   F   G

The names of all the notes on the staff look like this:

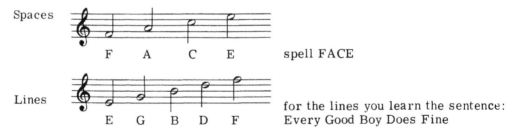

Spaces   F   A   C   E   spell FACE

Lines   E   G   B   D   F   for the lines you learn the sentence: Every Good Boy Does Fine

Sharps and Flats a sharp before a note (♯) raises the note one half step (one fret to the right) a flat before a note (♭) lowers the note one half step (one fret to the left).

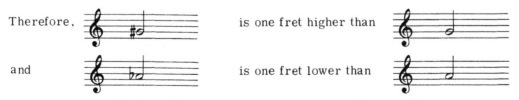

Therefore,   is one fret higher than

and   is one fret lower than

II. Rhythm — The notes most commonly found in music and the number of beats they receive are as follows:

♩ = quarter note = 1 beat

𝅗𝅥 = half note = 2 beats

𝅝 = whole note = 4 beats

𝅗𝅥. = dotted half note = 3 beats

♩. = dotted quarter note = 1½ beats

♪ = eight note = ½ beat

♬ = sixteenth note = ¼ beat

More than one eighth note may be beamed like this: ♫ or 𝅘𝅥𝅮𝅘𝅥𝅮

Also, more than one sixteenth note may be beamed like this: 𝅘𝅥𝅯𝅘𝅥𝅯𝅘𝅥𝅯𝅘𝅥𝅯 or 𝅘𝅥𝅯𝅘𝅥𝅯𝅘𝅥𝅯𝅘𝅥𝅯

Rests take the place of notes. They indicate silence. 𝄽 = ♩ 𝄼 = 𝅗𝅥 𝄾 = ♪ 𝄻 = 𝅝

III. Key Signatures

At the beginning of many pieces of music you will find a sharp or a flat on the staff beside the clef sign:

These are key signatures and they tell us 1) that all F's are to be played as F-sharp in the piece; 2) all B's are to be played as B-flat in the piece 3) all F's and C's and G's are to be played as Sharps in the piece to follow.

This shorthand saves the writer from having to write every sharp or flat into the music; and it makes it easier for you, once you understand the system, that is. Sometimes you will see this sign (♮) in the music: It is called a Natural sign. It cancels out a sharp or a flat and makes the note a regular B or F.

IV. Tuning Your Guitar

All the songs in this book use "G Tuning" on the DOBRO
The 6th string is tuned to a low G on the piano:

the 5th to a B:
the 4th to a D:
the 3rd to a G:
the 2nd to a B:
and the 1st to a D:

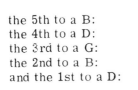

This is the tuning we will use in playing our DOBROS If you don't have a piano handy; another method of tuning your Dobro is as follows:

1) Tune the 6th string in unison to a low G on a piano (or tune to a pitch pipe)
2) Place the bar at the 4th fret of the 6th string. This will give you the tone or pitch of the 5th string. (B)
3) Place the bar on the 3rd fret of the 5th string to get the pitch of the 4th string. (D)
4) Place the bar on the 5th fret of the 4th string to get the pitch of the 3rd string. (G)
5) Place the bar on the 4th fret of the 3rd string to get the pitch of the 2nd string. (B)
6) Place the bar on the 3rd fret of the 2nd string to get the pitch of the 1st string. (D)

Strings

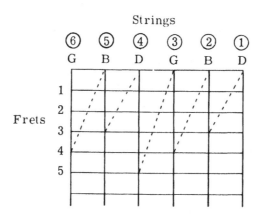

Frets

You may find when you are finished tuning your guitar the first time that it doesn't sound in tune to your ears (the tuned DOBRO should sound a G chord when played open). There is no easy way to learn the fine art of tuning your guitar. Only practice at it will sharpen your ear so keep trying!

We are getting close to being ready to play. You will need 2 metal finger picks and one plastic thumbpick. You will also need a metal bar. They come in several shapes and sizes. You should start with one that is big enough to hang on to and work your way down to a bar that is small enough to handle easily after you've played awhile. Some DOBRO players prefer round bars (shorter versions of the types used on pedal steel guitars), while others use a bar with a hollowed-out space for gripping it more firmly. You should decide for yourself which kind you like best.

You can use a pocket knife or a harmonica or a bottleneck or even a wrist pin from a car engine. All these have served in the past!

To aid you in finding your place in the music, tabulature notation will be used in addition to regular notes. Tab shows you which frets and strings to use while you pick.

The numbers in tablature indicate the fret to be played, and the line on which the number sits tells the string.

1st string
2nd string
3rd string
4th string
5th string
6th string

so a G major chord using all 6 strings played open would look like this:

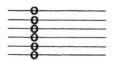

6

RHYTHM

One of the hardest of the elements of music for the beginner to master is rhythm - sometimes called "timing". If there is a deficiency in a musician's rhythmic training, it often remains a problem even after many years of playing. There are many difficult rhythms in this book. If you are not secure in your rhythm, then a careful study of it would be definitely in order.

The basic notes and their values in $\frac{4}{4}$ time are as follows:

o	= Whole note	= 4 beats
♩.	= Dotted half note	= 3 beats
♩	= Half note	= 2 beats
♩	= Quarter note	= 1 beat
♪	= Eighth note	= 1 2 beat
♪	= Sixteenth note	= 1 4 beat

Eighth notes often appear in groups of two and are beamed like this: ♫

Sixteenth notes often appear in groups of four and are beamed like this: ♬♬

A dot after a note makes the note 1 1 2 times longer than in would be otherwise. Example:

♩. = 1 1 2 beats

♩. = 3 beats

♪. = 3 4 beat

Triplets are three notes played in the time of two.
For example:

An eighth note triplet ($\overset{3}{\overline{♩♩♩}}$) receives the same amount of time as two

eighth notes (♫), that is one beat.

A quarter note triplet ($\overset{3}{\overline{♩ ♩ ♩}}$) receives the same amount of time as two

quarter notes (♩ ♩), that is two beats.

SPECIAL TECHNIQUES

Slides

Slides are played by striking a note and then sliding either up or down to another note without restriking the string. Slides are the most common special technique found in this book. The indication for a Slide in the music will be "SL".

Example:

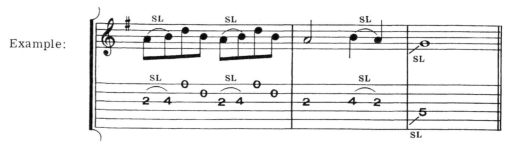

Hammer-on

Hammering-on is played by striking an open string and then hitting the bar down hard on a fret position of the same string, sounding a second note. The effect is often that of a slur, though not the same sound you get with a slide. The indication for a Hammer-on in the music will be "H".

Example:

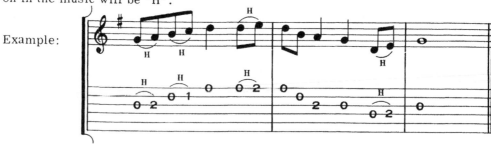

Pull-Off

Pulling-off is played by striking a note and then forcibly pulling the bar off the string, exposing a lower open note. The indication for a Pull-off in the music will be "P".

Example:

HOW TO HOLD THE DOBRO GUITAR

SITTING

STANDING

photos by Jim Cooper

THE DOBRO GUITAR

PARTS OF THE GUITAR

1. HEAD

2. TUNING KEYS

3. NUT (higher than on Spanish style guitar)

4. FRETS

5. NECK

6. INLAY POSITION MARKERS

7. SOUND HOLES (covered by screens)

8. BRIDGE

9. BODY

10. RESONATOR COVER PLATE

11. TAIL PIECE

photos by Jim Cooper

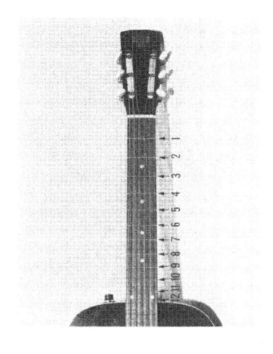

THE FRETBOARD
(showing fret numbers)

STAINLESS STEEL BAR
TWO STEEL OR PLASTIC FINGER-
PICKS PLASTIC THUMBPICK

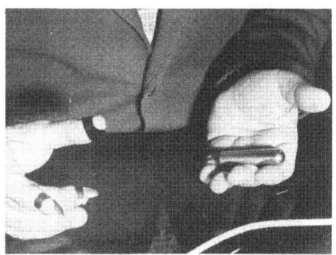

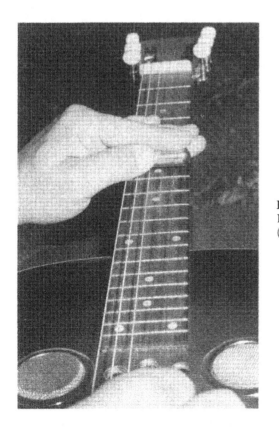

LEFT HAND POSITION, WITH
BAR IN BARRED POSITION
(flat on strings)

photos by Jim Cooper

BAR IN THE TIPPED POSITION

RIGHT HAND POSITION

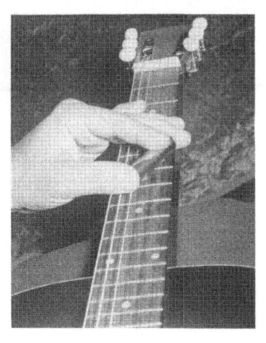

REVERSE SLANT

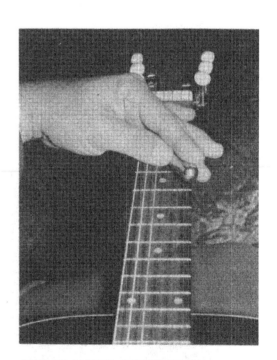

THE SLANTED POSITION

photos by Jim Cooper

12

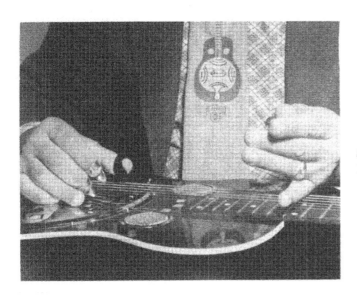

SIMPLE HARMONICS AT THE
12TH FRET

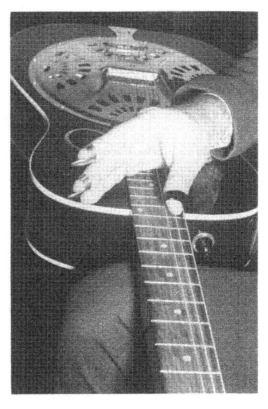

HAND POSITIONS FOR PALM
HARMONICS (note that the
palm of the right hand touches
the strings as the pick strikes
the strings.)

photos by Jim Cooper

OPEN G MAJOR CHORD

D MAJOR CHORD
(Bar at Seventh Fret)

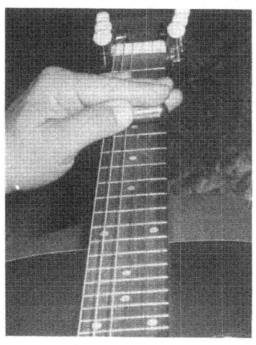

C MAJOR CHORD
(Bar at Fifth Fret)

photos by Jim Cooper

14

HARMONICS OR CHIMES

Harmonics are the beautiful bell-like tones that can be played on any stringed instrument. Left hand harmonics are played by touching the fourth finger of the left hand lightly at the 12th fret (G Chord), 7th fret (D chord), 19th fret (D Chord), 5th fret (G Chord), or 24th fret (G Chord), and picking the strings you desire. You may place the finger flat or use the tip. The finger may be lifted from the string when you pick, or left lying lightly on the string. So-called "false harmonics" may be produced in the same manner at other frets, but the volume is poor.

Palm harmonics are played by touching the heel of the right hand 12 frets (one octave) above the open or the barred fret and picking with the thumb pick. The right hand must be lifted immediately after picking the harmonic.

Finger harmonics are played in a manner similar to palm harmonics. The right thumb bends to about one inch from the palm of the right hand, and the tip of your finger (3rd finger preferred) touches the string lightly as you pick with the thumb. Much practice is required to master these techniques, so good luck and have fun.

BARRING CHORDS
ON THE FINGERBOARD

The chart below will show you where to find chords on the neck of the Dobro tuned to G. All these chords will be major. On the following pages we will show you how to play minors and seventh chords. Notice that some chords have two names, like A# or B-flat. This is common, and you need to learn both names for the frets.

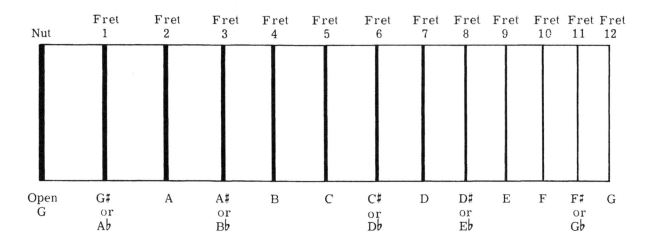

Nut	Fret 1	Fret 2	Fret 3	Fret 4	Fret 5	Fret 6	Fret 7	Fret 8	Fret 9	Fret 10	Fret 11	Fret 12
Open G	G# or Ab	A	A# or Bb	B	C	C# or Db	D	D# or Eb	E	F	F# or Gb	G

We have included only twelve frets on the chart because after 11, the chord names begin to repeat themselves. Therefore, 12 is G, 13 is G# or A-flat, 14 is A, etc. Thus by subtracting 12 frets from any high note you can discover the name of the chord; for example, subtracting 12 from the chord played on the 17th fret will give you the 5th fret, or C.

MINOR AND SEVENTH CHORDS

In regular G tuning, as used in this book, it is possible to play only major chords when barring the neck at any given fret and playing all six strings. This does not mean that minors and sevenths are impossible, but it is necessary to do some picking and choosing of strings being played in order to get the right chord.

It takes a careful study of music theory to determine exactly which notes to play to give you the chords listed below. Anyone interested in knowing the "whys" can consult a music theory book. But for now, let us give you the benefit of our years' experience and list several Non-Major chords and how to play them. Most of these are not full three-note chords but just two of the three notes. They will sound more like the real thing when you play with another instrument using full chords, like a guitar or mandolin or piano.

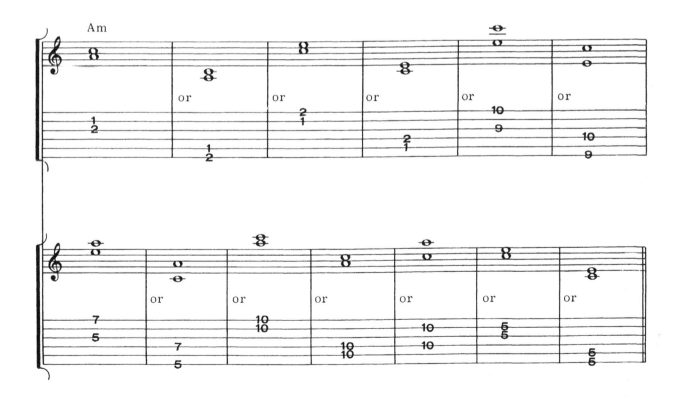

Bb minor

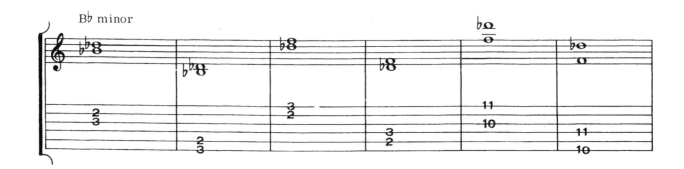

B minor

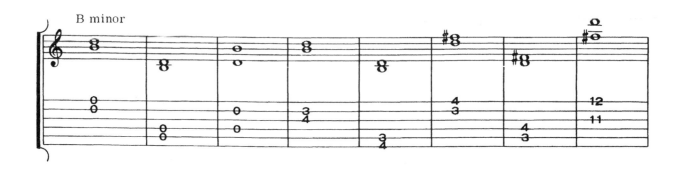

18

C minor

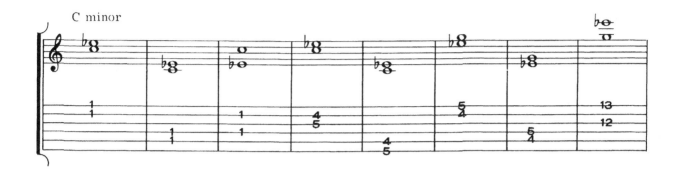

C# minor

D minor

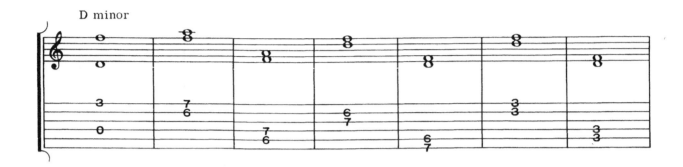

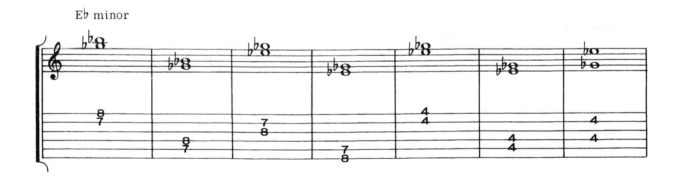

Eb minor

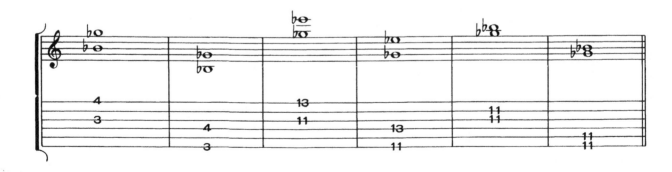

20

E minor

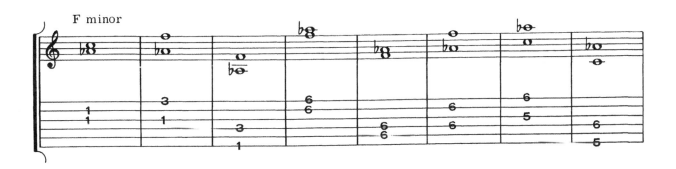

F minor

21

F# minor

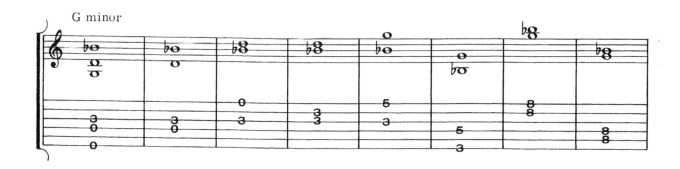

G minor

22

G# minor

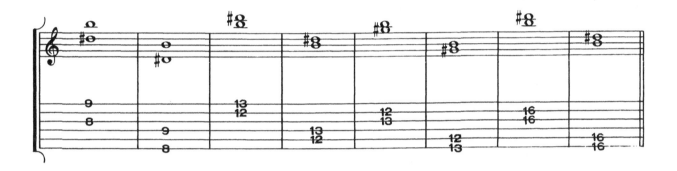

In the higher positions, using the proper steel bar, you can play 3-string minor chords:

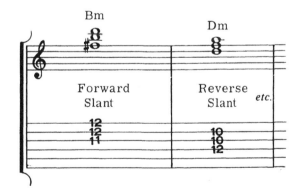

Seventh chords can be implied in G Tuning by playing the 1st and 2nd strings (or the 4th and 5th strings) 3 frets higher than the chord is normally played on the fingerboard of the Dobro. Sounds confusing, but it's easy to do, and the effect is great!

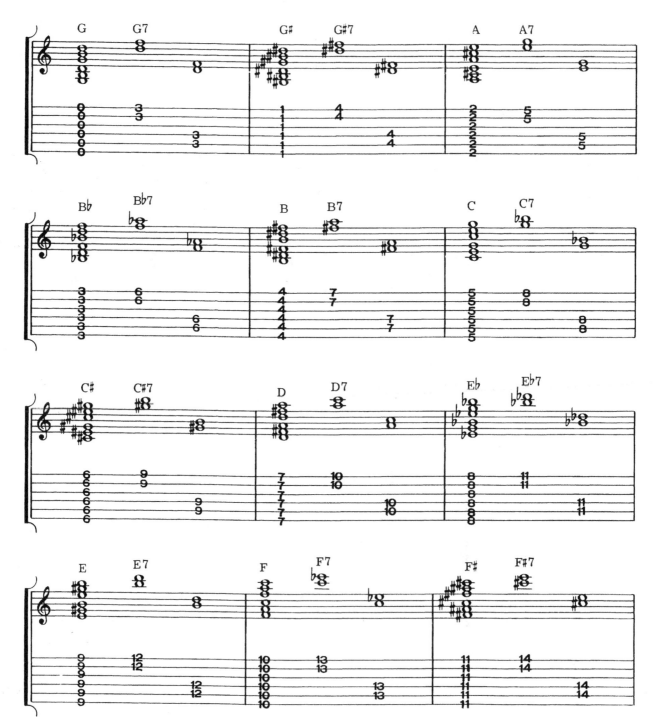

24

The seventh chords on the preceding page are often played as tremolos, sliding out of the major chord, like this:

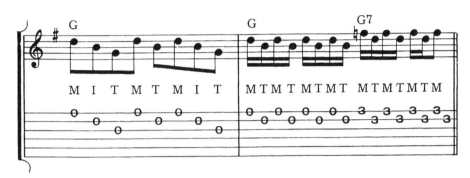

There are many other seventh chord positions possible on the DOBRO, but the above will do well for you in the beginning. Some, but by no means <u>all</u>, of the seventh chords are:

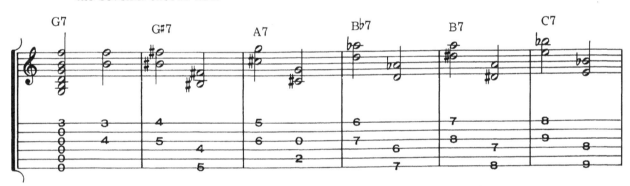

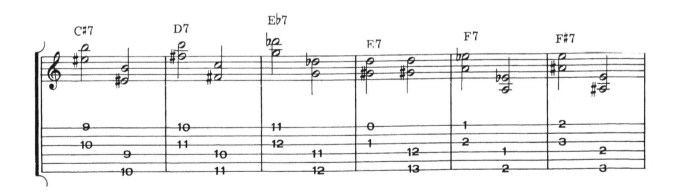

RIGHT HAND PICKING

There are two main styles of right hand picking on the DOBRO: the Hawaiian style and the Three-Finger Roll style. This book uses both ways of playing, since any good DOBRO player uses both in his or her playing. We have included right hand finger indications to aid you in working out the songs in this book. These are not hard and fast: you may vary them to suit your own taste and needs, but for many people who work on this book, the right hand indications will be of great assistance in trying to understand the often complex nature of Bluegrass Dobro.

We indicate the Thumb with a "T", the Index Finger with "I" and the Middle Finger with "M". If the letters appear over each other, then they should be played together. Sometimes the thumb will strum several strings at once.

An additional word about the two styles found in this book. If we may attempt to stereotype them in order to try to show the differences between the two styles, we can say that the Hawaiian style puts the melody on the first string most often (played by the middle finger) and tends to supply both the melody and some chordal accompaniment at the same time. The Three-Finger Roll style, based in large part on the banjo rolls made famous by Earl Scruggs, tends to rely on the rapid succession of note patterns, with the melody being present often in the Thumb. In this style of playing, the melody needs to be accented a little in order that it be heard distinctly over the other fill- in notes of the right hand. Both styles require a lot of practice, and as we mention above, the great DOBRO players are equally competent in both styles. We hope you will achieve success in your own playing.

Tom Swatzell with his metal body Dobro.

BILE 'EM CABBAGE DOWN

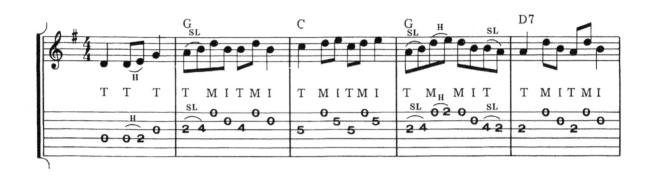

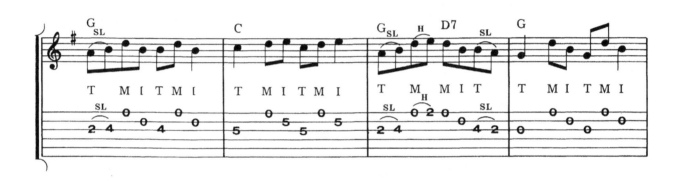

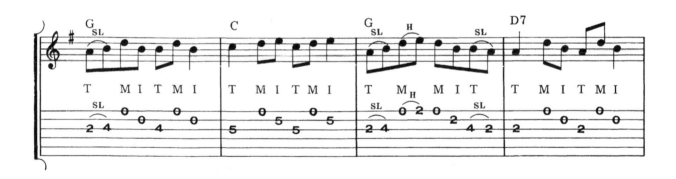

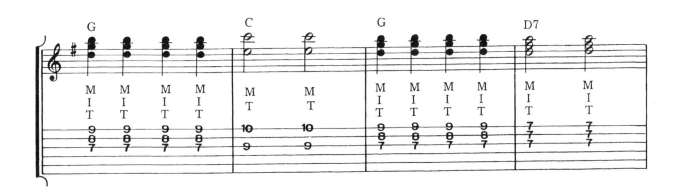

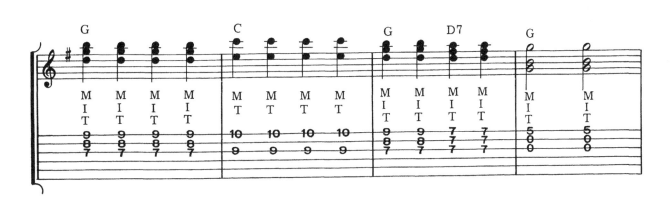

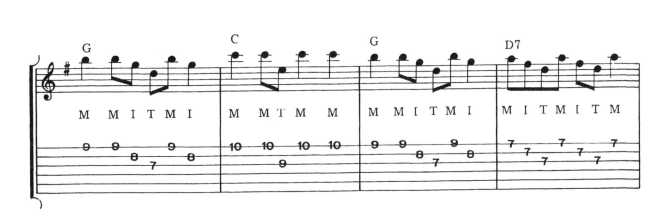

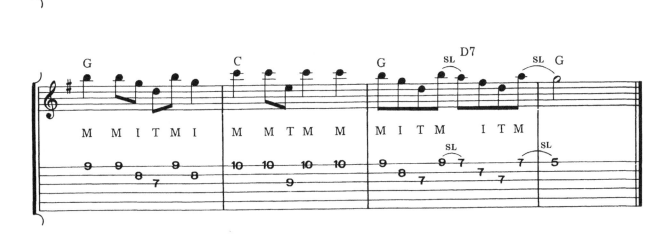

SHADY GROVE

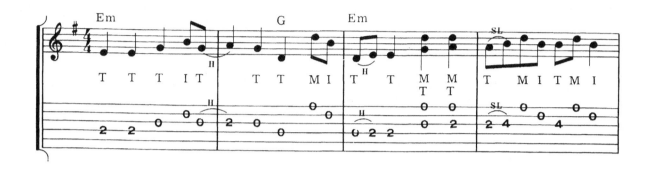

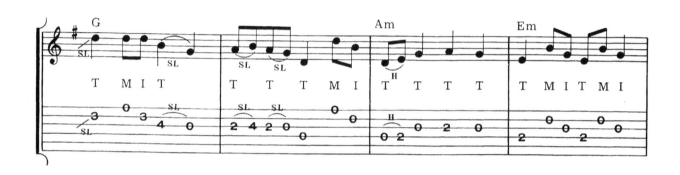

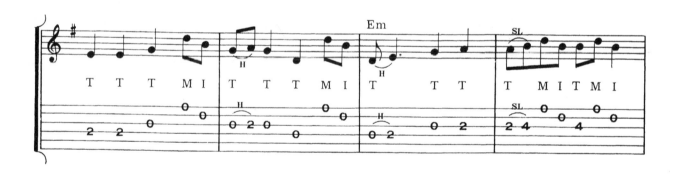

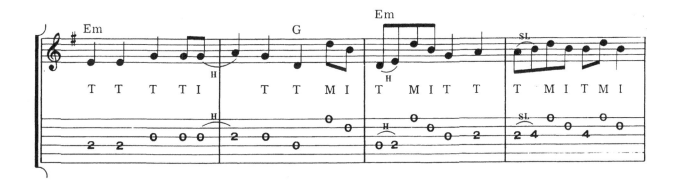

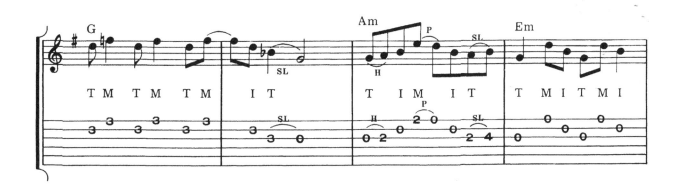

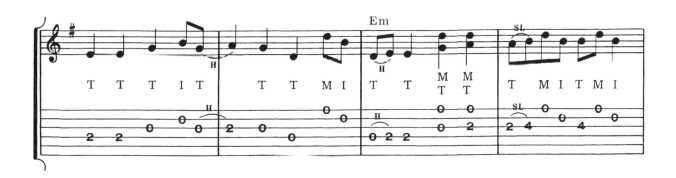

HOW BEAUTIFUL HEAVEN MUST BE

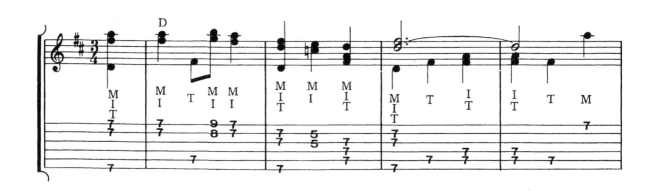

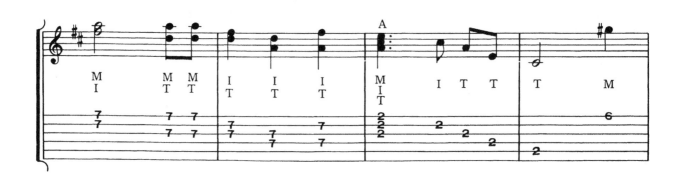

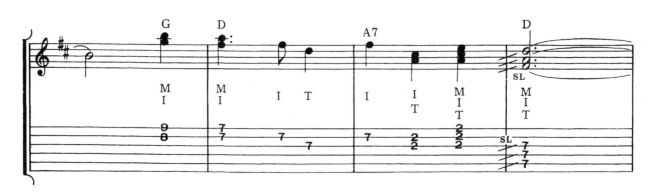

33

PASS ME NOT

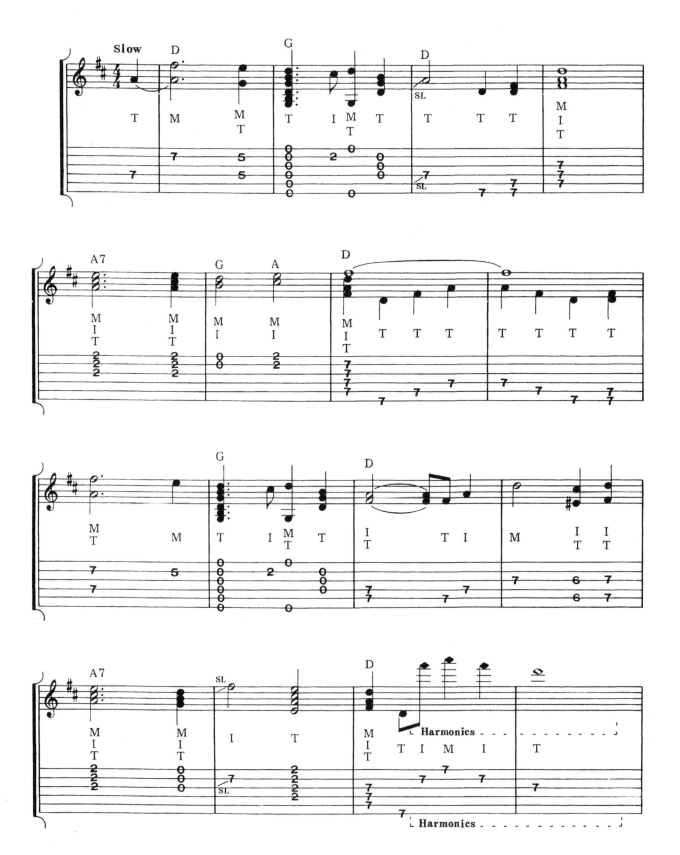

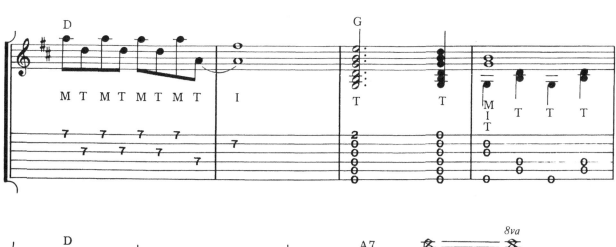

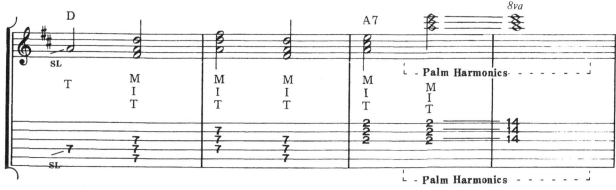

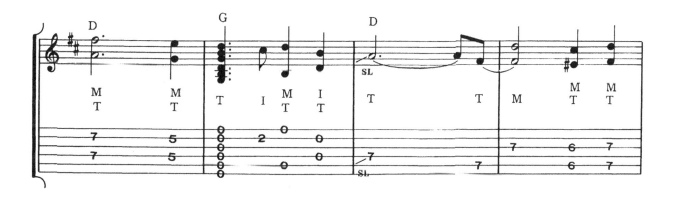

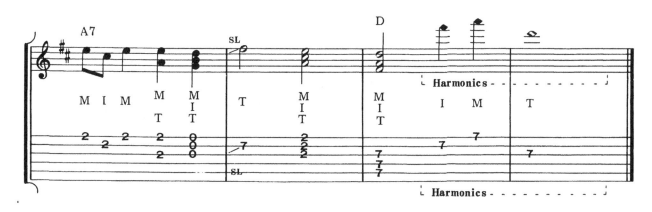

JOHN HARDY

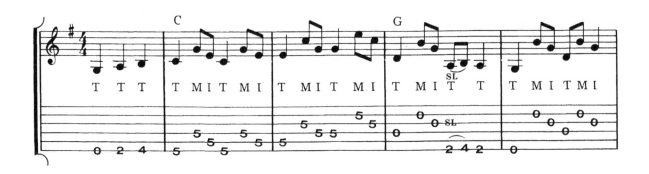

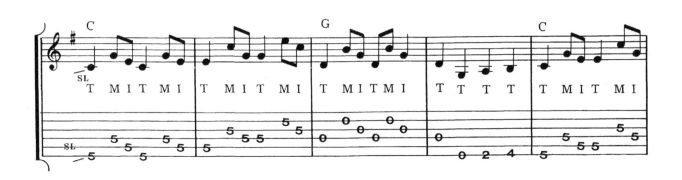

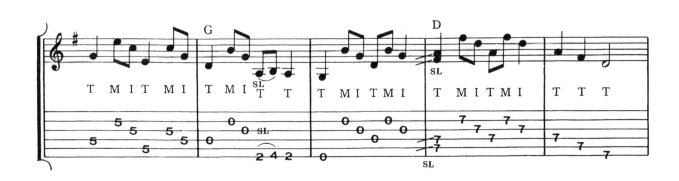

37

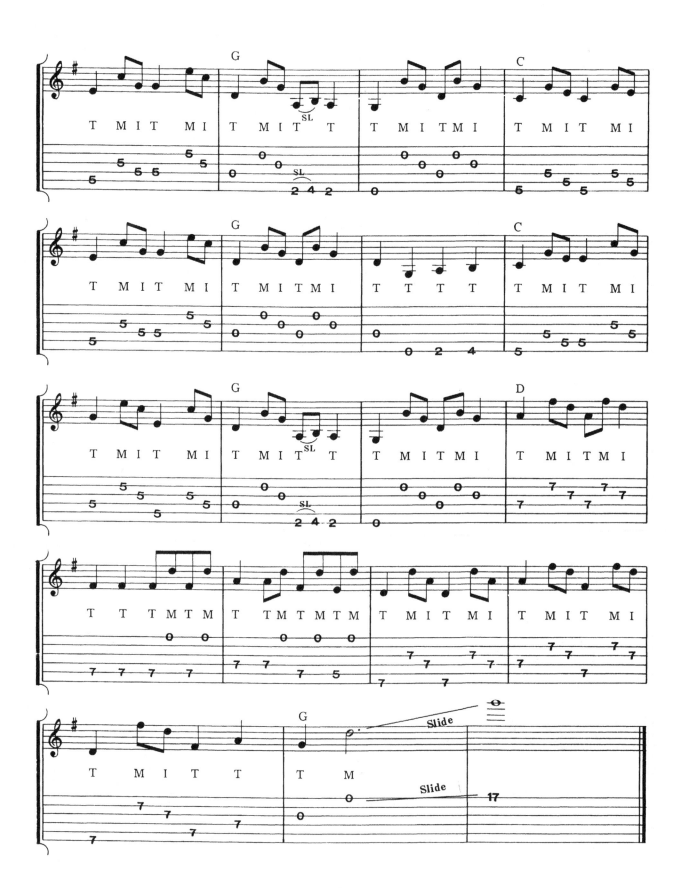

OH SUSANNAH

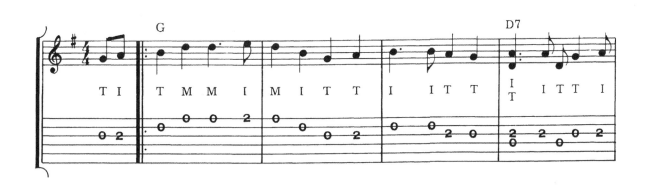

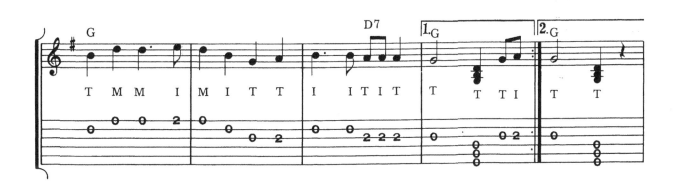

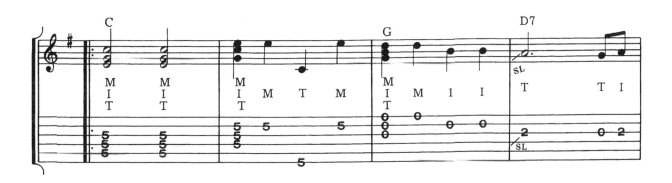

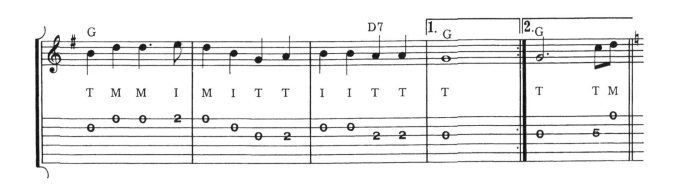

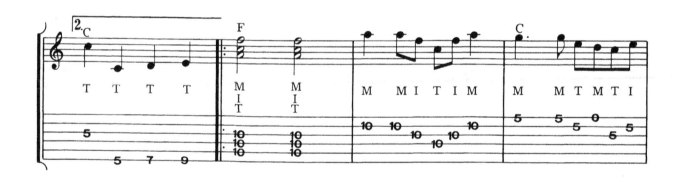

STREETS OF LAREDO

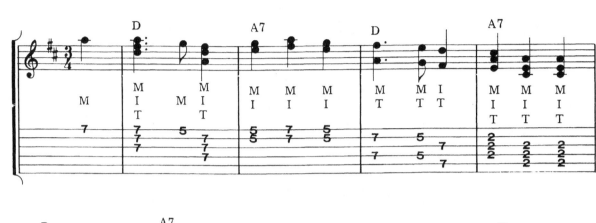

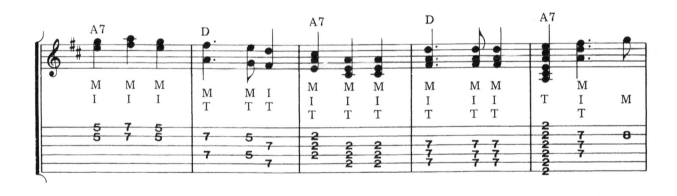

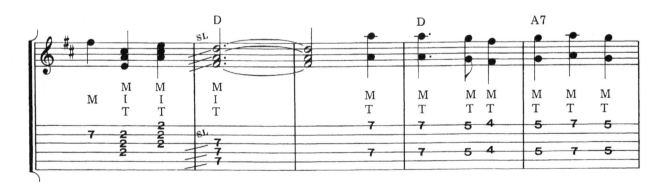

43

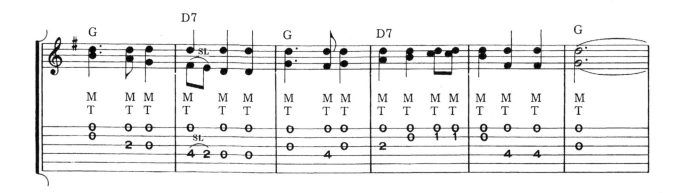

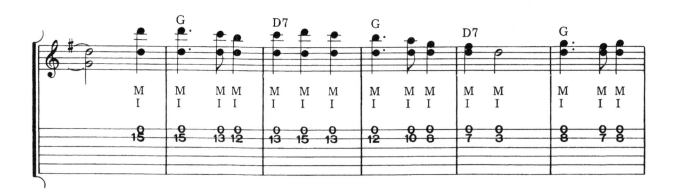

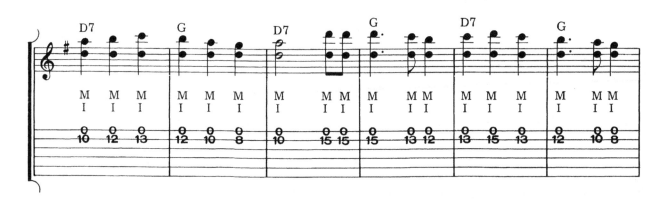

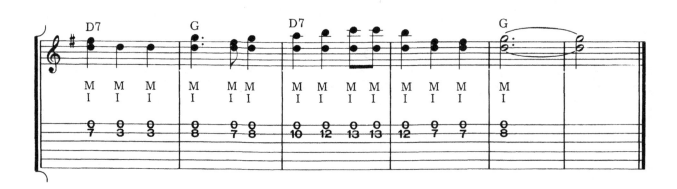

Tom Swatzell—"Have Dobro, Will Travel."

TRAIL TO MEXICO

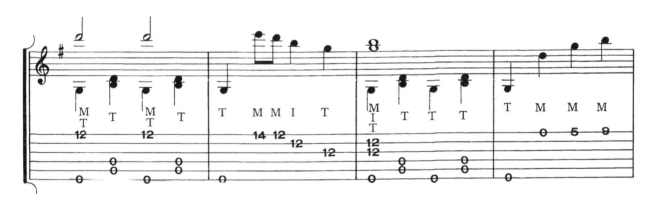

BELIEVE ME, IF ALL THOSE
ENDEARING YOUNG CHARMS

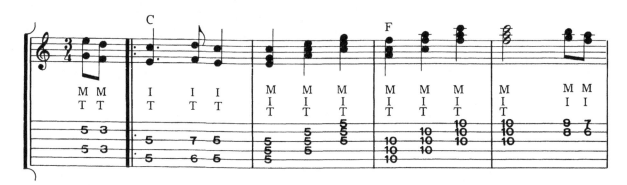

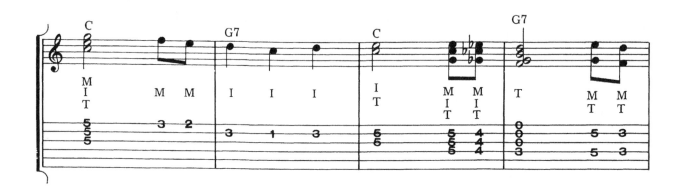

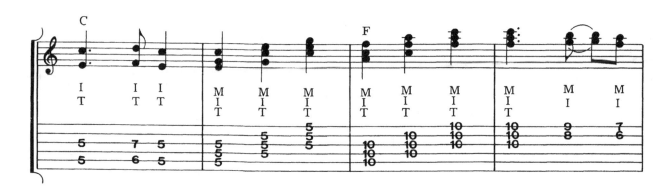

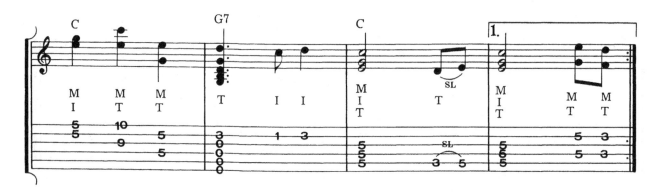

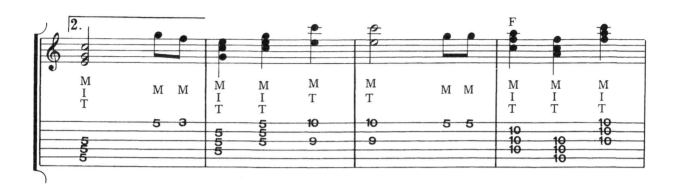

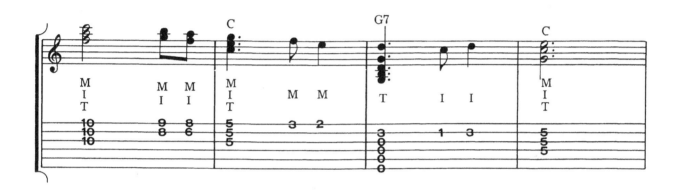

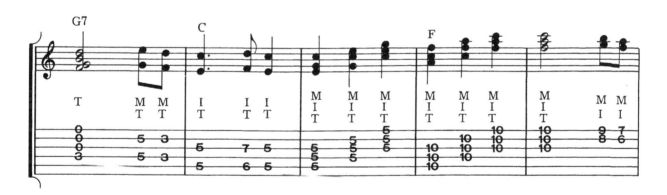

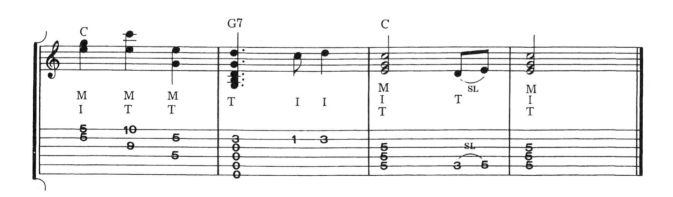

SOURWOOD MOUNTAIN

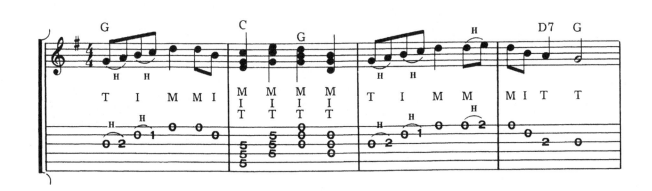

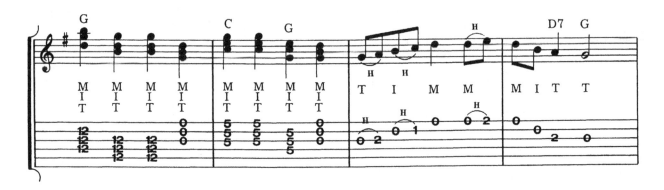

GROUND HOG

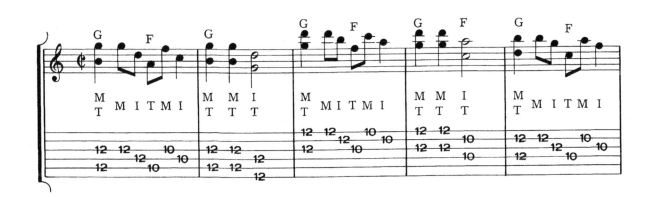

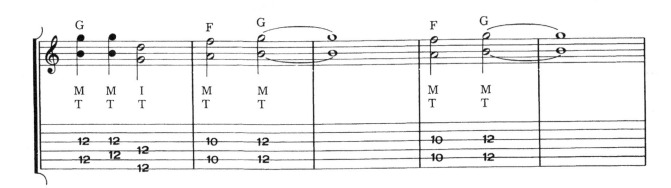

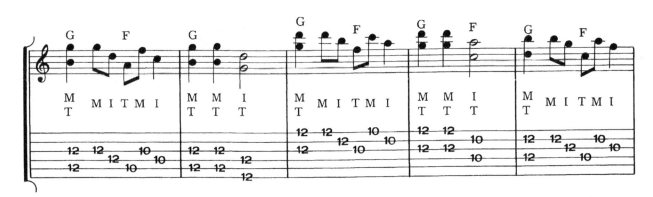

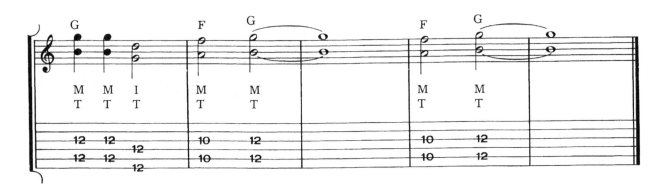

Tom Swatzell and his collection of fancy Dobros.

BURY ME BENEATH THE WILLOW

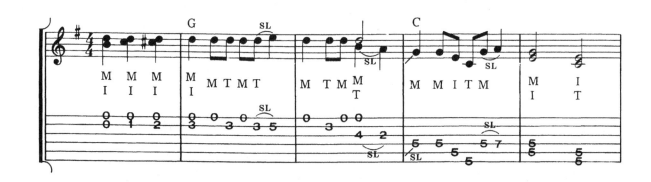

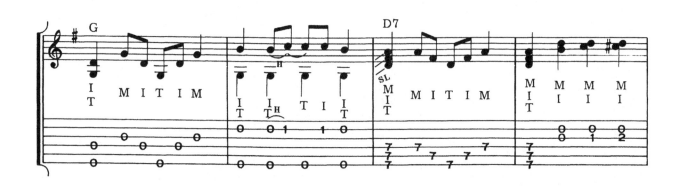

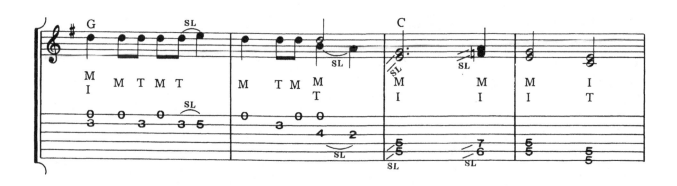

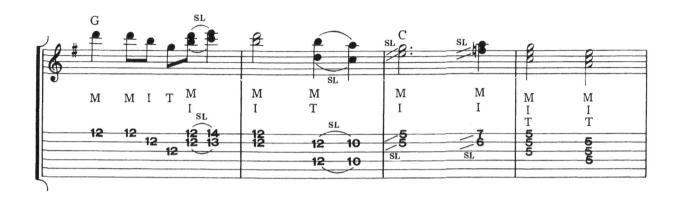
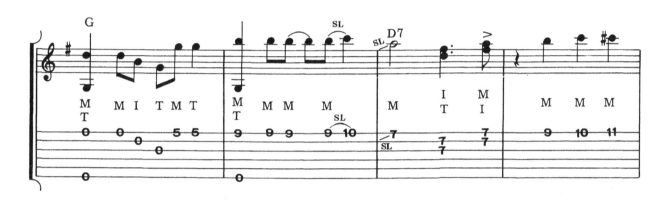
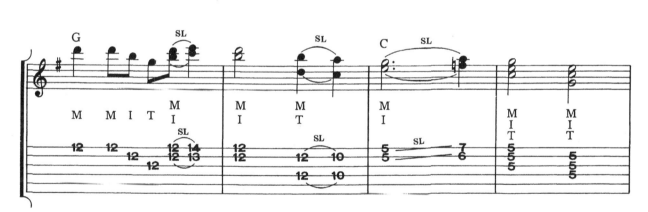
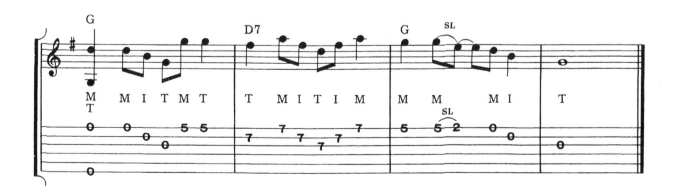

CRIPPLE CREEK

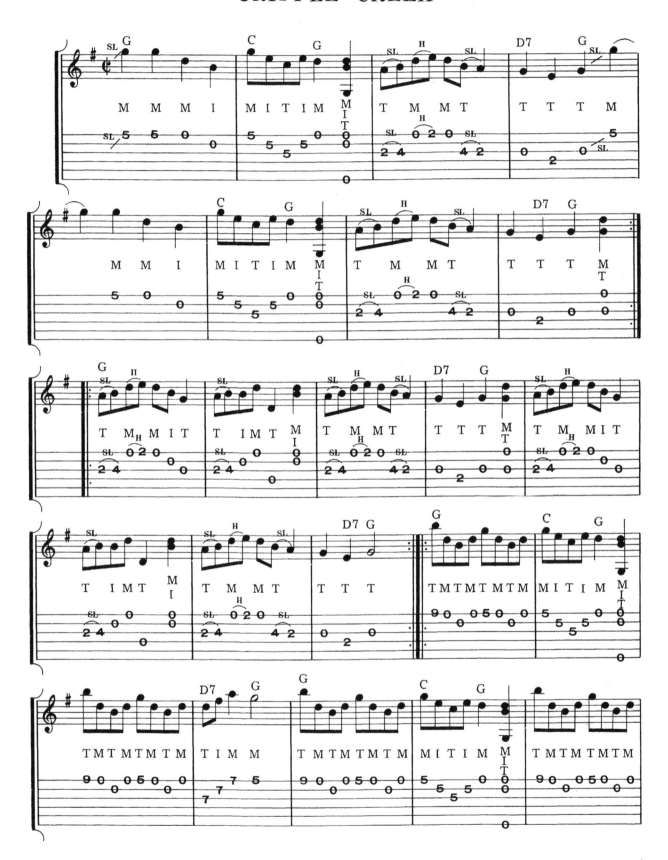

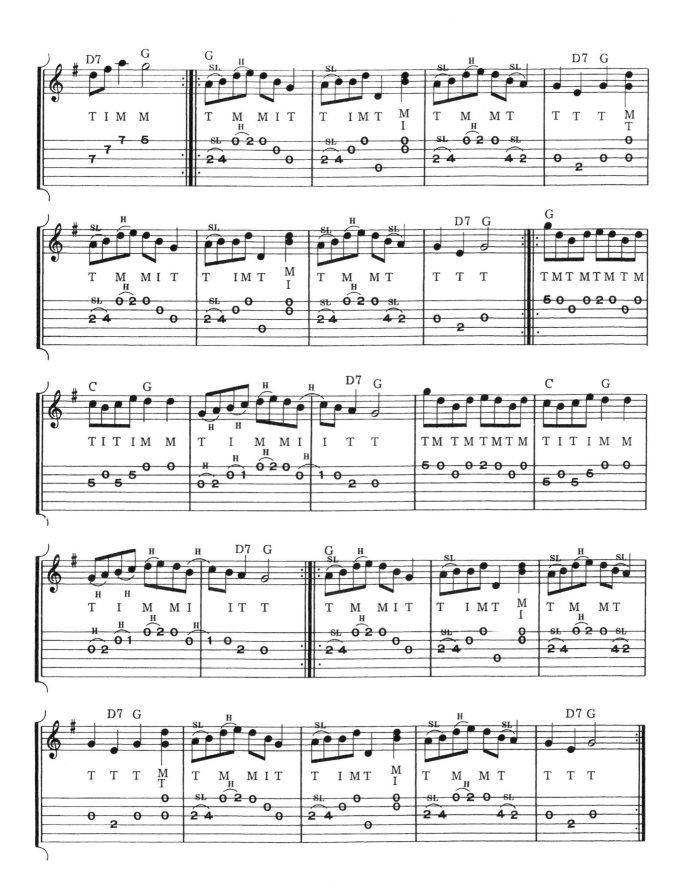

LIFE'S RAILWAY TO HEAVEN

59

SEEING NELLIE HOME

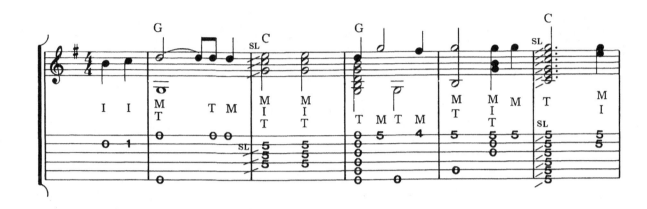

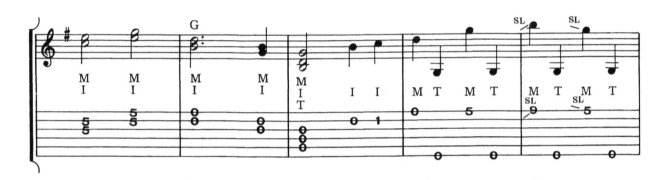

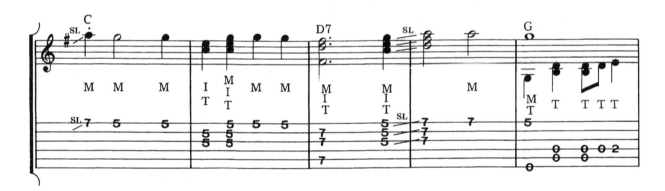

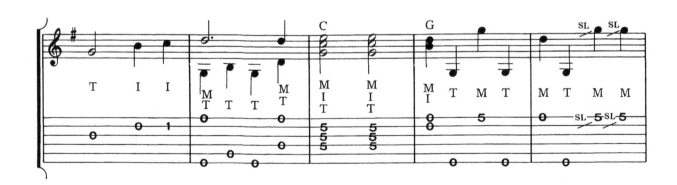

62

Tom Swatzell

LITTLE BROWN JUG

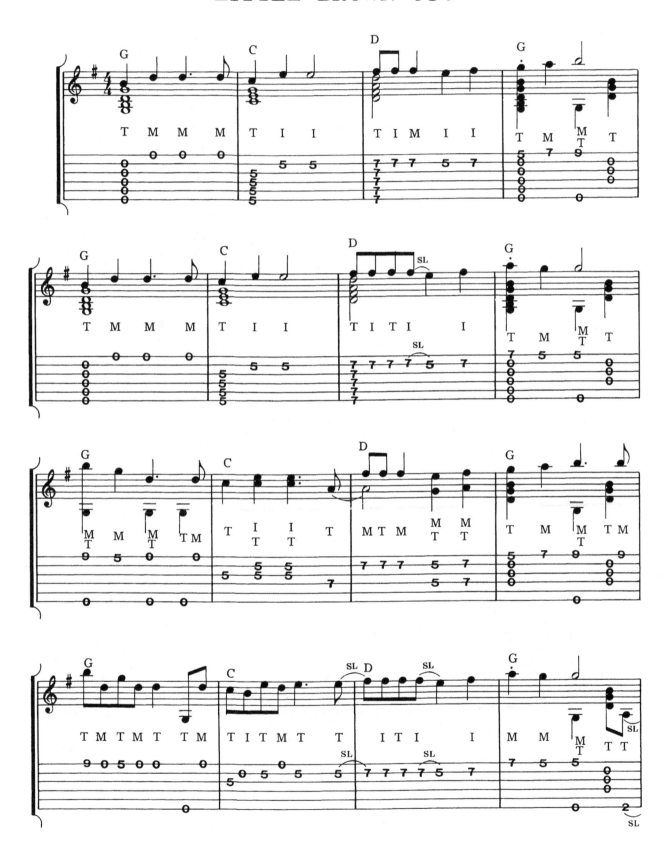

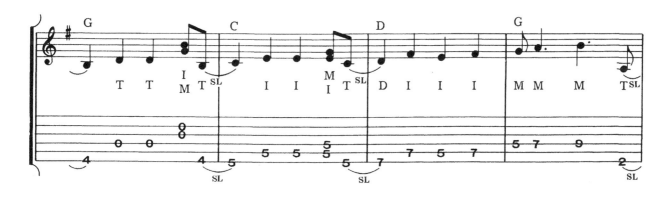

BANKS OF THE OHIO

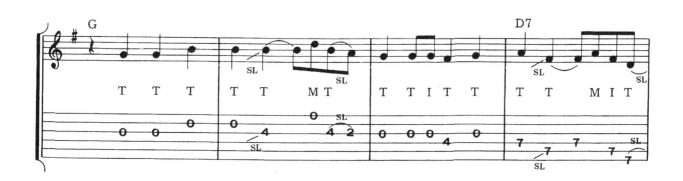

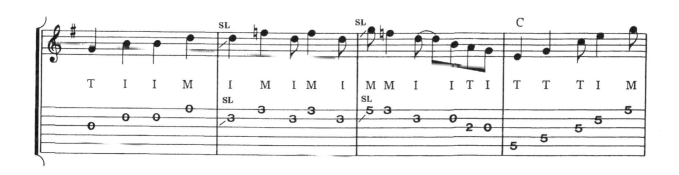

JUST A CLOSER WALK WITH THEE

DEVIL'S DREAM

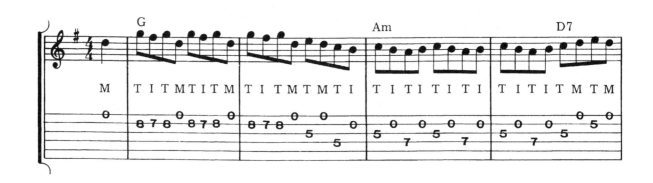

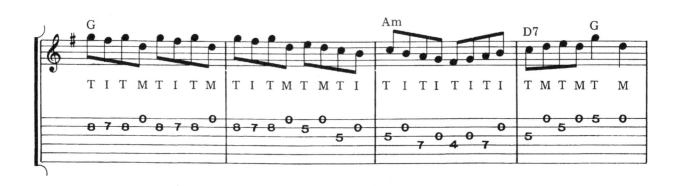

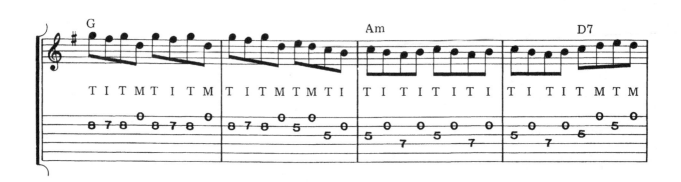

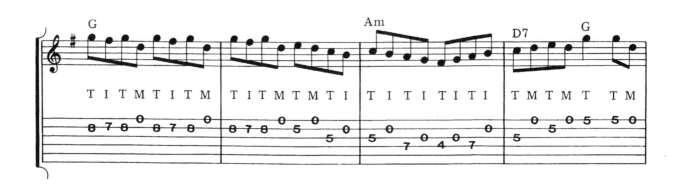

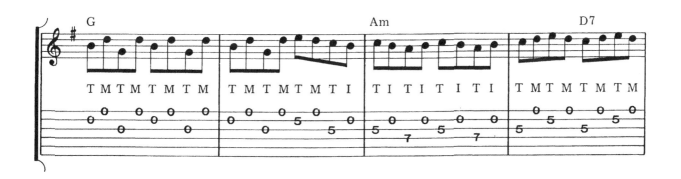

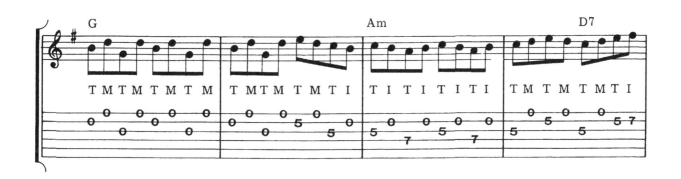

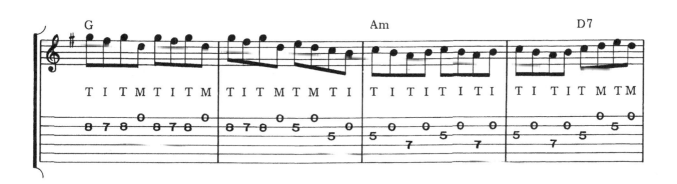

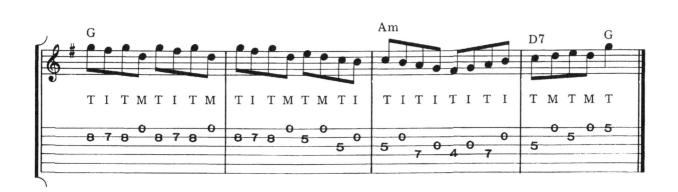

BLUES FOR BIG JOHN

© Copyright 1982, Kenneth G. Eidson

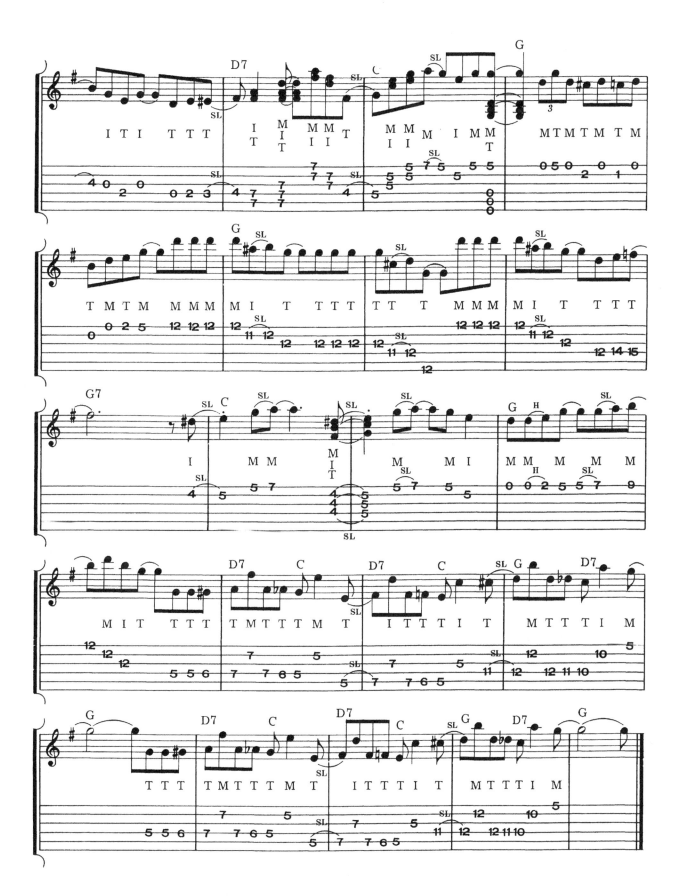

BLACKBERRY BLOSSOM

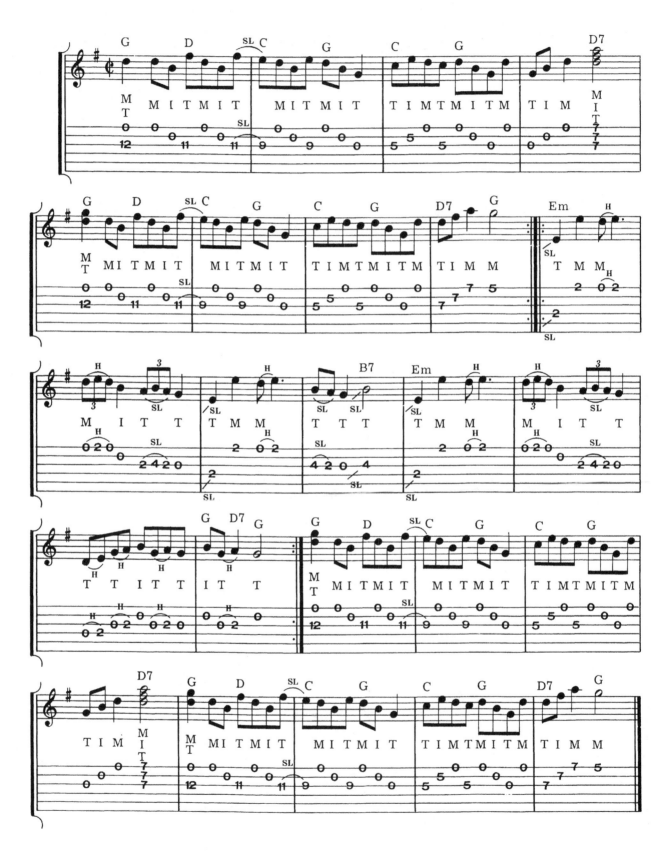

Dobro—model 1000

AMAZING GRACE

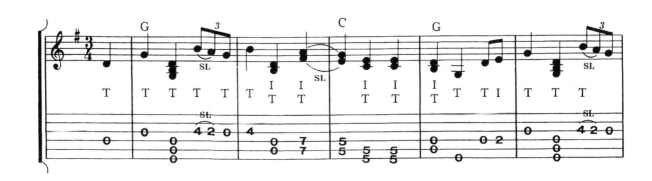

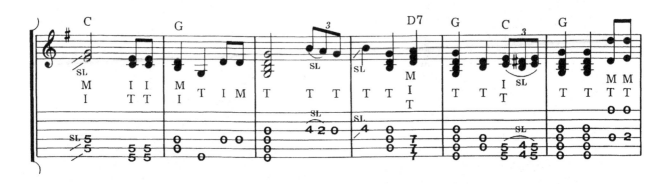

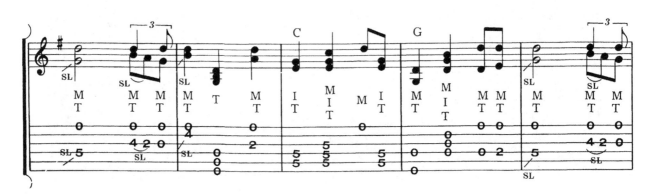

GOIN' DOWN THAT ROAD FEELIN' BAD

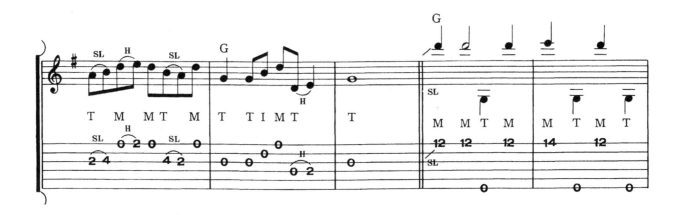

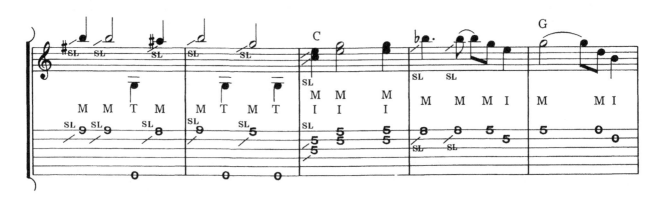

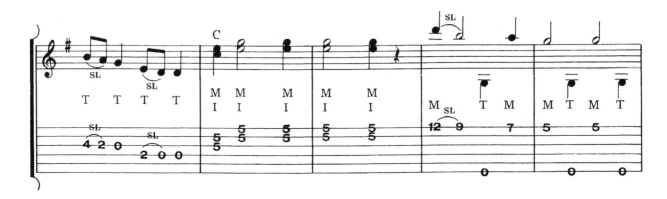

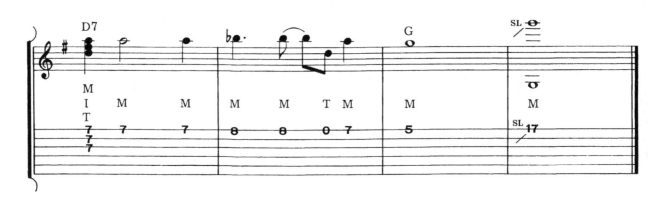

Notice the license plate!!

FLOP EARED MULE

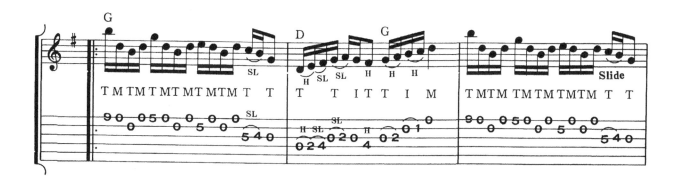

LISTEN TO THE MOCKING BIRD

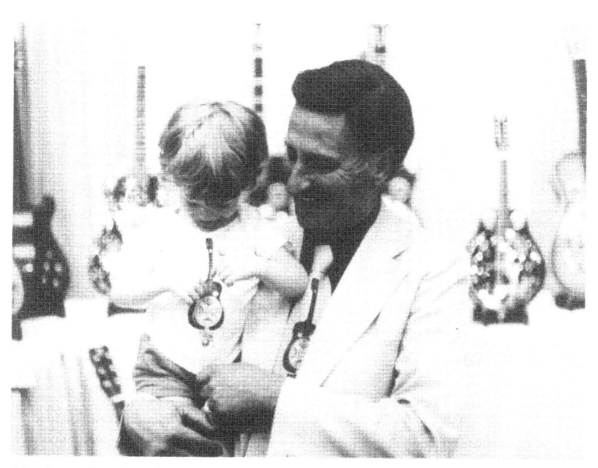

Tom Swatzell and grandson, Bill Eidson.

Alphabetical Listing of Tunes

Made in United States
North Haven, CT
30 November 2022

27476335R00050